Table of Contents

Humbleness, Meekness

I do not believe that anybody has all the answers, after all, we are human! I do however believe that everybody should be humble and meek, so that we can learn all there is to learn from the Holy Spirit, the Word of God, and from each other. My goal with writing this book is to spread information. Please do your own research, pray for answers and ask questions if you have any, and please read this book with an open mind and open heart. May God be with you.

Psalm 25:9 The meek will he guide in judgment: and the meek will he teach his way.

James 4:6 But he giveth more grace. Wherefore he saith, God resisteth the proud, but giveth grace unto the humble.

James 1:5 If any of you lack wisdom, let him ask of God, that giveth to all men liberally,

and upbraideth not; and it shall be given him.

Acts 17:11 These were more noble than those in Thessalonica, in that they received the word with all readiness of mind, <u>and searched the scriptures daily, whether those things were so.</u>

Please always have discernment when it comes to Biblical studies. Anyone can teach anything by leaving out Bible verses. My goal is not to deceive anyone but to share God's Good News.

The Bible has been translated into English from its original Hebrew and Greek versions.
All verses on these pages are from the King James Version Bible.

John 1:1 In the beginning was the Word, and the Word was with God, and the Word was God.

Introduction to Biblical Feasts

What Biblical Feasts are we to keep as followers of Christ? First, I want to define what it means to be a Christian, a follower of Christ.

Christian: follower of Christ, trying to do as He does.

1 Peter 2:21 For even hereunto were ye called: because Christ also suffered for us, leaving us an example, that ye should follow his steps:

I think the keyword is "trying". All we can do, as imperfect sinners, is do our best, and try. God's grace helps us to not sin. God's grace allows us to try our best to be Holy, and when we inevitably mess up because we are imperfect, we are forgiven. It really is a beautiful thing.

So, what feasts did Christ, our Messiah, keep? We know that Christ did not come to destroy the law but fulfill it.

Matthew 5:

17 Think not that I am come to destroy the law, or the prophets: <u>I am not come to destroy</u>, but to fulfill.

18 For verily I say unto you, Till heaven and earth pass, one jot or one tittle shall in no wise pass from the law, till all be fulfilled.

19 Whosoever therefore shall break one of these <u>least commandments</u>, and shall teach men so, he shall be called the least in the kingdom of heaven: but whosoever shall do

and teach them, the same shall be called

great in the kingdom of heaven.

He fulfilled everything that was said and done by the law and prophets, by being the Word in human form. He was the prophecies fulfilled, and He sanctified us in the eyes of the Lord. The law could not, and will never be able to sanctify us, because as humans, we have evil in our hearts. We fail and hurt people and ourselves. We sin. We break the law. That is why we need Christ. Because the wages of sin is death, we could only be redeemed by Christ's innocent blood. Christ is perfect. He is sinless. He is someone who never broke a commandment of God.

1 John 3:4 Whosoever committeth sin

transgresseth also the law: for sin is the

transgression of the law.

Christ kept Passover. We also know that He taught and healed on the Sabbath. He kept Passover with the disciples, which is famously called, "The Last Supper". In

Luke 22:7-8, He told the disciples to kill the Passover

Lamb so that they could eat it together. After their Passover

dinner is when Communion took place, and the ceremony

of feet washing. It was during this time Christ commanded

us to continue to take Communion. Personally, I honor

Communion with whoever I am celebrating Passover with.

We also wash each other's feet and read the scriptures of

this teaching. The fact that He kept Passover Ordinances

and honored it implies that He probably would have kept

the other Biblical Feasts. Old Testament Feasts prophecy

the New Testament.

The Holy Feasts were given to the Israelites by God

through Moses. Most people have been taught that the Old

Testament is irrelevant to our salvation and our modern

world. That is just not true. Remember, we are living in the

last days in a broken world, and Satan is busy deceiving

people.

Matthew 24:24 For there shall arise false Christs, and false prophets, and shall shew great signs and wonders; insomuch that, <u>if it were possible</u>, they shall deceive the very elect.

Revelation 12:9 And the great dragon was cast out, that old serpent, called the Devil, and Satan, which deceiveth the whole world: he was cast out into the earth, and his angels were cast out with him.

As followers of Christ, we should aim to do as He did. One part of that process is learning about the Feasts of the Lord and trying to keep them ourselves

Spring Feasts

Passover is the first Holy Feast of the year. It is celebrated in Spring. In **Leviticus 23** we are commanded by God to keep Passover in the first month on the 14th day at even. "Even", simply means when the sun is even with the earth. A day starts at sunset, since first there was darkness when the Lord was creating the world.

The Biblical year is followed by the phases of the moon.

Isaiah 66:23 And it shall come to pass, that from one new moon to another, and from one sabbath to another, shall all flesh come to worship before me, saith the LORD.

Historically a new moon signifies a new month. Because a new moon cycle is only about 29.5 days, every 2–3 years is a "Jewish Leap Year". It has 13 moons instead of 12, so there is an extra month added to the calendar. The extra month is called Adar Aleph, and then the month of Adar is referred to as Adar Bet during a leap year. A Jewish leap year will happen 7 times in a 19-year cycle. The last Jewish leap year was 2022. The Biblical calendar is even reflected in our modern, Western calendar. September, October, November, and December all start with numerical prefixes. September comes from the Latin word "septem" meaning "seven" for example. October, November, and December also come from Latin words meaning "eight", "nine", and "ten". Since December is the 10th month (if you determine the months using those numerical prefixes of the names of those months), that makes January the 11th month, and February the 12th. We need to pay attention to the new moon that appears in March, because generally that is the start of the Biblical New Year. Also, you will notice, in the northern hemisphere of the world, where Jerusalem is located, that March is typically when the earth starts dethawing, temperatures start rising, and the first growths of the season start to spring up. The modern most widely accepted and used Jewish calendar says that <u>Pesach</u> (Hebrew word for Passover) starts this year (2023) on the evening of April 5, 2023. If the March new moon happens on March 21 before sundown, then sundown marks the 1st day of the New Year. The 14th day is 2 weeks later, starting at sundown on the 4th, and ending at sundown on the 5th. This is the start of the Pesach feast week.

There are many different calendars however, because the Bible tells us exactly when to celebrate but not how to exactly determine the start of the new year. Each Biblical calendar relies on signs of the seasons and cultural determinations. The best that we can do is try our best. Our world is broken, lost and confused because of Satan and worldwide deception everywhere. Pray and use discernment when researching and determining your own Biblical calendar for your family.

Even of April 5 -Lord's Passover

dinner and Communion

-Starts the Feast of

Unleavened Bread

"<u>Chag HaMatzot</u>"-Happy Unleavened Bread

"<u>Chag Pesach Sameach</u>" -Happy Passover

Festival

Leviticus 23:5 In the fourteenth day of the

first month <u>at even</u> is the LORD'S Passover.

Exodus 34:

18 The feast of unleavened bread shalt thou

keep. Seven days thou shalt eat unleavened

bread, as I commanded thee, in the time of

the month Abib: for in the month Abib, thou

camest out from Egypt.

22 And thou shalt observe the feast of weeks,

of the first fruits of wheat harvest, and the

feast of ingathering at the year's end.

The children of Israel were commanded in

Leviticus 23:10 to give an offering of first fruits when

they came into the Promised Land and reaped their first

harvest. Then, God commands them on the day after that

Shabbat (Hebrew word for Sabbath) to count 7 Shabbats

and give another offering. This second holy convocation

and offering commanded in **Leviticus 23** is known as

the Feast of Weeks (7 Shabbats-50 days- "Pentecost"

comes from a Greek word meaning "fifty").

Christ was prophesied by these feasts, in Passover,

He was the Passover Lamb. His blood protects us from

eternal death by spiritually covering us, the way the

Israelites covered their doorposts in lamb's blood during the original Passover. He rose from the dead 3 days later, on the day after the Sabbath. Christ was the "first fruit" of God's work that was being done through Him. During communion which was started by Christ, we eat the blood and flesh of Him. We do that regularly by reading the gospel and filling ourselves with the Word of God. Also, leaven may be symbolic of sin. We are commanded to purge the sin out of our houses and bodies during this time. Christ helped us to overcome sin. We were freed from the slavery that was sin!

In **John 19:34**, scripture tells us that when Mashiach's (Hebrew word for Christ's) side was pierced, blood AND water came out of Him. So, when I prepare my communion cup, I use water mixed with juice (wine). Water has been used Biblically in connection with baptism and remitting of sin, cleansing, healing, and life.

John 4:14 Christ gives us water that gives eternal

life.

Matthew 14:25 Christ walked on water, He is

God and has dominion over life and death.

John 2:9 He turned water into wine, His blood is

mixed with the living Word.

John 3:5 Water baptism is the birth to new life.

Mark 16:9 Now when Jesus was risen

early the <u>first day</u> of the week, he appeared

first to Mary Magdalene, out of whom he

had cast seven devils.

John 6:

50 This is the bread which cometh

down from heaven, that a man may eat

thereof, and not die.

51 I am the living bread which came down from heaven: if any man eat of this bread, he shall live for ever: and the bread that I will give is my flesh, which I will give for the life of the world.

52 The Jews therefore strove among themselves, saying, How can this man give us his flesh to eat?

53 Then Jesus said unto them, Verily, verily, I say unto you, Except ye eat the flesh of the Son of man, and drink his blood, ye have no life in you.

54 Whoso eateth my flesh, and drinketh my

blood, hath eternal life; and I will raise him

up at the last day.

55 For my flesh is meat indeed, and my

blood is drink indeed.

56 He that eateth my flesh, and drinketh my

blood, dwelleth in me, and I in him.

57 As the living Father hath sent me, and I

live by the Father: so he that eateth me, even

he shall live by me.

58 This is that bread which came down from

heaven: not as your fathers did eat manna,

and are dead: he that eateth of this bread

shall live for ever.

He was the Promised Land. He is the Holy Gift sent

from God.

50 Days after Christ's resurrection the disciples

honored the command of **Leviticus 23:21** to have a

holy convocation (convocation is another word for holy

meeting) and were given the gift of the Holy Ghost. This is

known as Pentecost. In Hebrew, the Feast of Weeks is

called <u>Shavuot</u>, which means "weeks".

The world celebrates Pentecost 7 weeks after Easter

which has roots in Paganism. I would encourage anyone

reading this and seeking truth to do their own research on

Easter and consider not celebrating it. The Lord calls us to

be set apart from paganism and a light to the world.

If we celebrate Shavuot according to Passover's

date and the New Testament example, in 2023 it would fall

on the "even" of May 27, 2023.

Now that you know how to calculate and find the

start and end dates of these feasts on your own, you must

know how to keep them. There are many ordinances, so remember to try your best because the Lord knows your heart and do not be too hard on yourself if you cannot keep the feast day ordinances perfectly. We are not perfect beings. When we celebrate these days with Him, it brings us closer to Him and grows us spiritually. These are His Holy Days, so we should try to keep them His Way.

Numbers 9:14 And if a stranger shall sojourn among you, and will keep the passover unto the LORD; according to the ordinance of the passover, and according to the manner thereof, so shall he do: ye shall have one ordinance, both for the stranger, and for him that was born in the land.

Exodus 12

- On the 10th day of the month, we are commanded to pick a lamb that we will eat for our household size. If your house is too small for a whole lamb, you should share with another family if possible. For example, I am not able to do this because I do not have access to livestock so I try to visit a local butcher shop on this day and buy a lamb roast. Remember, these commands were written to ancient Israelites and in modern times and places may be difficult to follow exactly.

- On the 14th day, it is to be (humanely) killed in front of the congregation. We are to do this in the evening, shortly before sundown to prepare and cook the meat for the Passover meal.

- Take the blood, and smear it on the outside of the door frame of wherever you are eating.

- Roast it over a fire if possible, we use our indoor modern oven.

- Eat it with unleavened bread and bitter herbs. Some examples are horseradish, parsley, sage, and coriander seeds.

- Eat it only that night and any leftovers burn with fire. I recommend getting a very small amount of lamb to reduce waste, especially if you do not have access to a fire.

- Do not eat it raw or sodden with water.

- If you are roasting it over a fire, keep its head and legs intact, leave its body intact.

- Eat it in haste, which means in a hurry with your shoes on, similar to how the ancient Israelites had to prepare to depart from Egypt. It is a memorial service.

- Do not work on the 1st day of the feast, and the last.

- On the first day, clean out all the leaven from your house and eat no leaven for the remainder of the feast. We try to vacuum, dust, and clean out our pantry and meal plan. We try to avoid restaurants and fast food for the week. We also avoid all leavening agents such as yeast, baking powder, baking soda, cream of tartar, bicarbonates, phosphorus, phosphate, beer, sourdough, soda and carbonated drinks.

- Do not leave the building you ate the Passover meal in until morning.

- Only the circumcised in heart (believers) should eat the Passover meal.

- Keep it only in your house, do not travel with the lamb. Do not break any of its bones.

- Every generation must keep this feast.

- Do not even carry anything leavened.

Deuteronomy 16:4

- Passover must happen the same night as
  communion. **1 Corinthians 11:23**

My Personal Checklist for Passover and Communion

1. Put blood on the door.

2. Eat with bitter herbs and unleavened bread.

3. Burn any leftovers by morning.

4. Eat with loins girded, shoes on, eat in haste.

5. Don't go outside until morning.

6. Blow trumpet (shofar) because it is a celebration and Holy Feast.

7. Read Order of Service

8. After supper, break bread and drink wine (Communion).

9. Give thanks.

10. Feet washing ceremony.

Super Simple Unleavened Bread Recipe

- 2 cups of flour

- 1 cup of water

Bind with a fork, then add a little more water. Use your hand to mix and flour the counter, knead the dough for 5 minutes. Divide into golf ball shapes and flatten. Cook in pan-no oil needed. Wait for air pockets to appear then it is done.

Fall Feasts

The Spring Feasts prophecy the Mashiach's first coming, while the Fall Feasts are more focused on the "harvest" time spiritually. The first Fall Holy Feast of <u>Yah</u> (a name for God- **Psalms 68:4**) is the Feast of Trumpets. The Feast of Trumpets in Hebrew is called <u>Yom Teruah</u>.

Leviticus 23:

24 Speak unto the children of Israel, saying, In the seventh month, in the first day of the month, shall ye have a sabbath, a memorial of blowing of trumpets, an holy convocation.

25 Ye shall do no servile work therein: but ye shall offer an offering made by fire unto the LORD.

No work is to be done on this day, and we are to congregate and blow trumpets (<u>shofars</u>). According to my calculation, the Feast of Trumpets starts at sundown, September 14th. The blowing of trumpets will happen when Christ returns to earth at His 2nd coming. It is an honor to keep this feast and be reminded of our hope.

1 Thessalonians 4:

16 For the Lord himself shall descend from heaven with a shout, with the voice of the archangel, and with the trump of God: and the dead in Christ shall rise first:

17 Then we which are alive and remain shall be caught up together with them in the clouds, to meet the Lord in the air: and so shall we ever be with the Lord.

Next is the Day of Atonement. This is called <u>Yom Kippur</u> in Hebrew.

Leviticus 23:

27 Also on the tenth day of this seventh month there shall be a day of atonement: it shall be an holy convocation unto you; and ye shall afflict your souls, and offer an offering made by fire unto the LORD.

28 And ye shall do no work in that same day: for it is a day of atonement, to make an atonement for you before the LORD your God.

29 For whatsoever soul it be that shall not be afflicted in that same day, he shall be cut off from among his people.

30 And whatsoever soul it be that doeth any work in that same day, the same soul will I destroy from among his people.

31 Ye shall do no manner of work: it shall be a statute for ever throughout your generations in all your dwellings.

32 It shall be unto you a sabbath of rest, and ye shall afflict your souls: in the ninth day of the month at even, from even unto even, shall ye celebrate your sabbath.

No work at all is to be done on this day. We are to congregate on this day and "afflict our souls". Many people take this day to fast from both food and water. However, not to discourage anyone from fasting for the Lord, but when searching for the truth on the matter I found that the original word used for "afflict" means to humble yourself and be downcast. This day is for reminding ourselves of our sinful, evil nature, and remembering all that the Meshiach has done for us as He made the final atonement for our sins. In this year 2023, Yom Kippur falls on the even of September 24th.

The 7th and final Holy Celebration of the year is the Feast of Tabernacles. This is called <u>Sukkot</u> in Hebrew.

Leviticus 23:

34 Speak unto the children of Israel, saying, The fifteenth day of this seventh month shall

be the feast of tabernacles for seven days unto the LORD.

35 On the first day shall be an holy convocation: ye shall do no servile work therein.

36 Seven days ye shall offer an offering made by fire unto the LORD: on the eighth day shall be an holy convocation unto you; and ye shall offer an offering made by fire unto the LORD: it is a solemn assembly; and ye shall do no servile work therein.

39 Also in the fifteenth day of the seventh month, when ye have gathered in the fruit of the land, ye shall keep a feast unto the LORD

seven days: on the first day shall be a sabbath, and on the eighth day shall be a sabbath.

40 And ye shall take you on the first day the boughs of goodly trees, branches of palm trees, and the boughs of thick trees, and willows of the brook; and ye shall rejoice before the LORD your God seven days.

41 And ye shall keep it a feast unto the LORD seven days in the year. It shall be a statute for ever in your generations: ye shall celebrate it in the seventh month.

42 Ye shall dwell in booths seven days; all that are Israelites born shall dwell in booths:

43 That your generations may know that I made the children of Israel to dwell in booths, when I brought them out of the land of Egypt: I am the LORD your God.

44 And Moses declared unto the children of Israel the feasts of the LORD.

It says in verse **42** that all that are born Israel shall dwell in booths-from my understanding, if you are baptized you are born again as a child of God into His family. So if possible we should all try to keep the command of dwelling in booths for this feast. The way most believers do this is by going on a camping trip with your family and/or church congregation. No work is to be done the 1st and 8th day, and the whole time is to be a time of feasting and rejoicing! The Lord covered Israel through the wilderness while they dwelled in tents, and Christ covers us while we navigate through the last days. God is good!

The Biblical Feasts offer us a time to celebrate with the Lord and grow closer to Him. It is a chance to delve deeper into His ways and understand them. The Feasts refill us with hope, emotions, and love. Spiritual growth and learning happens. They are a very special time and we will keep them forever, even in Heaven with the Lord Himself.

Exodus 12:14 And this day shall be unto you for a memorial; and ye shall keep it a feast to the LORD throughout your generations; ye shall keep it a feast by an ordinance for ever.

The Sabbath and New Moon

Weekly Holy Day

Science shows we are at our best when we have at least 1 day of physical, mental, and emotional rest. The Sabbath is a day to put down house chores, errands, and work. I understand some jobs like doctors and nurses may not be able to get the Sabbath off of work, and God bless those people who do essential jobs! Christ said it is lawful to do good on the Sabbath. Most of us have work however that can afford to not be done at least 1 day a week, from sundown Friday until sundown Saturday. Personally, I try to do errands, cooking, meal prepping, and chores Friday before sundown if possible. Remember that Christ says the Sabbath was made for man. Use this day to recharge and spend time with God.

Matthew 12:

10 And, behold, there was a man which had his hand withered. And they asked him, saying, Is it lawful to heal on the sabbath days? that they might accuse him.

11 And he said unto them, What man shall there be among you, that shall have one sheep, and if it fall into a pit on the sabbath day, will he not lay hold on it, and lift it out?

12 How much then is a man better than a sheep? Wherefore it is lawful to do well on the sabbath days.

Christ taught in the synagogues on the Sabbath. We should try our best to congregate to worship, study the Word, and pray on the Sabbath. The ordinances of the Sabbath differ contextually in the Old Testament.

Exodus 35:3 tells us not to kindle a fire in our habitations. Some people believe we can light one before the Sabbath such as a candle, but not during. Some take that verse and decide not to use electricity in their homes, and others will not use their stove or microwave to cook. The ordinances I have found whether they are still to be applied or not, the individual should study.

2 Timothy 2:15 Study to shew thyself approved unto God, a workman that needeth not to be ashamed, rightly dividing the word of truth.

- **Nehemiah 10:31** Do not buy or sell.

- **Jeremiah 17:21-22** Bear no burden.

- **Psalms 81:2** Blow the trumpet.

- **Exodus 20:8-10** Do not work.

- **Hebrews 4:9-10** Rest.

- **Leviticus 23:3** Have a holy convocation.

- **Isaiah 58:13-14** Call the Sabbath a delight. Be selfless for God.

- **Exodus 35:3** Kindle no fire.

- **Leviticus 23:32** Sundown until sundown.

- **Nehemiah 8:11** Do not grieve.

The New Moon

A New Moon Biblically represents the start of a new month. This is how we calculate the time between the first month and the rest of the months to determine when the Holy Feasts are. We are commanded to blow the shofar

on a new moon, according to **Psalms 81:3**.

Birthdays, Easter, and Christmas

Modern holidays involve pagan traditions, which is why I encourage other believers to keep Biblical Feasts instead. For example, Easter is said to be a spring fertility holiday based around the goddess Ishtar (Eastar-Ishtar?). This is why people celebrate using bunny symbols, sweets and sugars, and eggs. In paganism, these things symbolize sex and fertility. Christmas is originally pagan also. The tradition of decking a tree with ornaments and metals and putting it in your house is part of a winter solstice ritual. See **Jeremiah 10**. When pagans were forced to accept Chrisitanity in Rome, they brought their pagan traditions along but disguised them as Christian by saying they were doing it for Jesus. We really do not know when Christ's birthday was, so to say it is a specific day is a lie. The devil is the Father of Lies. We should celebrate Christ's birth every day as Christians and always be thankful. Instead of keeping these modern pagan holidays, I choose to try to keep the Lord's Holy Feasts.

Biblically birthdays are only mentioned around heathenism and sin. I found 3 instances in the Bible when birthdays are mentioned. First, Pharaoh's birthday in **Genesis 40**. The chief baker was hung. Death. Second, in **Job 1**, scripture says that his sons and daughters feasted and celebrated their birthdays. Afterwards it says that Job had to sanctify them after their partying and sin. Thirdly, in **Mark 6** we read that King Herod had John the Baptist beheaded at his birthday celebration. Birthdays are a form of idolization of a certain individual. Personally, I am grateful for another year when it is my birthday, but I do not want others celebrating me. If they want to show me love and care, I believe they should do so any day of the year. Not just the day they are culturally pressured to do so.

Order of Service

<u>SHALOM</u> ! : Christ said "peace be unto you" so let us say **SHALOM** which is a greeting (or farewell) that means "peace" in Hebrew! (**John 20:19,21,26**).
In **Matthew 10:11-13** we are commanded to let our peace be upon a worthy house (see also; **Ephesians 6:23**), so let us say

Shabbat Shalom!

THE SHOFAR : The shofar must be

blown at any appointed time; the seventh day

(the Shabbat, or Sabbath), any feast <u>yome</u>

(day), or new moon. (**Psalm 81:3**) This is a

commandment of our <u>'elohim</u> (God) and a

statute for <u>Yashar'al</u> (Israel) forever. Let us

blow the shofar!

PRAISE AND PRAYER : Psalms

100:4 commands us to come before His courts

with praise! In **Matthew 21:15**, the children

were crying in the temple saying "Ho-sha`-na"

(Hosanna) to the son of Daweed (David) who is

Yahosha`**. In **Matthew 21:16 Yahosha` states

this is the perfect praise. We are assembled

before Him; therefore let us shout **"HO-SHA`-**

NA" YAHOSHA` !

The Bible has commanded His people to say the Hebrew word "Amein" (**Psalms 106:48**) which means "truly". Let us say "amein"!

**SHEMA`** : One cannot obey the commandments if one does not listen or pay attention to Yah's (**Psalms 68:4**) Word. One must shema`, which means to hear intelligently or understand and obey.

SHEMA`, O YASHAR'AL : Let us read.

Deuteronomy 6, King James Version

<u>1</u> Now these are the commandments, the statutes, and the judgments, which the Lord

your God commanded to teach you, that ye might do them in the land whither ye go to possess it: 2 That thou mightest fear the Lord thy God, to keep all his statutes and his commandments, which I command thee, thou, and thy son, and thy son's son, all the days of thy life; and that thy days may be prolonged. 3 Hear therefore, O Israel, and observe to do it; that it may be well with thee, and that ye may increase mightily, as the Lord God of thy fathers hath promised thee, in the land that floweth with milk and honey. 4 Hear, O Israel: The Lord our God is one Lord: 5 And thou shalt love the Lord thy God with all thine heart, and with all thy soul, and with all thy might. 6

And these words, which I command thee this day, shall be in thine heart: 7 And thou shalt teach them diligently unto thy children, and shalt talk of them when thou sittest in thine house, and when thou walkest by the way, and when thou liest down, and when thou risest up. 8 And thou shalt bind them for a sign upon thine hand, and they shall be as frontlets between thine eyes.9 And thou shalt write them upon the posts of thy house, and on thy gates. 10 And it shall be, when the Lord thy God shall have brought thee into the land which he sware unto thy fathers, to Abraham, to Isaac, and to Jacob, to give thee great and goodly cities, which thou buildedst not, 11 And houses full of all good things, which thou filledst not, and wells digged, which thou diggedst not, vineyards and olive trees, which thou plantedst not; when thou shalt have eaten and be full; 12 Then beware lest thou forget the Lord, which brought thee forth out of the land of Egypt, from the house of bondage. 13 Thou shalt fear the Lord thy God, and serve him, and shalt swear by his name. 14 Ye shall not go after other gods, of the gods of the people which are round about you; 15 (For the Lord thy God is a jealous God among you) lest the anger of the Lord thy God be kindled against thee, and destroy thee from off the face of the earth.

<u>16</u> Ye shall not tempt the Lord your God, as ye tempted him in Massah. <u>17</u> Ye shall diligently keep the commandments of the Lord your God, and his testimonies, and his statutes, which he hath commanded thee. <u>18</u> And thou shalt do that which is right and good in the sight of the Lord: that it may be well with thee, and that thou mayest go in and possess the good land which the Lord sware unto thy fathers. <u>19</u> To cast out all thine enemies from before thee, as the Lord hath spoken. <u>20</u> And when thy son asketh thee in time to come, saying, What mean the testimonies, and the statutes, and the judgments, which the Lord our God hath commanded you? <u>21</u> Then thou shalt say unto

thy son, We were Pharaoh's bondmen in Egypt;

and the Lord brought us out of Egypt with a

mighty hand: 22 And the Lord shewed signs

and wonders, great and sore, upon Egypt, upon

Pharaoh, and upon all his household, before our

eyes: 23 And he brought us out from thence,

that he might bring us in, to give us the land

which he sware unto our fathers. 24 And the

Lord commanded us to do all these statutes, to

fear the Lord our God, for our good always,

that he might preserve us alive, as it is at this

day. 25 And it shall be our righteousness, if we

observe to do all these commandments before

the Lord our God, as he hath commanded us.

THE TEN

COMMANDMENTS : The Ten

Commandments located in **Exodus** chapter **20,** is a list of laws or "covenant", which means agreement between 'el (God) and His people. It is so important that it is the only thing 'el wrote with His own hand for man (**Exodus 24:12**), without which man is unable to learn the way of holiness, which is the whole duty of man (**Ecclesiastes 12:13**) forever (**Matthew 5:17-18, 19:16-19**). Therefore, we should remind ourselves of them. (**Psalm 1:2, 37:30-31, 40:8**). In **Isaiah 58:13-14**, Yah told His people to delight in the Sabbath, and He will cause them to ride on the high places of the Earth.

Psalms 119:174 says the law is a delight so we should delight in it (law) to get the full blessings! Let us read.

Exodus 20:1-17, King James Version

1 And God spake all these words, saying, 2 I am the Lord thy God, which have brought thee out of the land of Egypt, out of the house of bondage. 3 Thou shalt have no other gods before me. 4 Thou shalt not make unto thee any graven image, or any likeness of any thing that is in heaven above, or that is in the earth beneath, or that is in the water under the earth.

5 Thou shalt not bow down thyself to them, nor serve them: for I the Lord thy God am a jealous

God, visiting the iniquity of the fathers upon the children unto the third and fourth generation of them that hate me; 6 And shewing mercy unto thousands of them that love me, and keep my commandments. 7 Thou shalt not take the name of the Lord thy God in vain; for the Lord will not hold him guiltless that taketh his name in vain. 8 Remember the sabbath day, to keep it holy. 9 Six days shalt thou labour, and do all thy work: 10 But the seventh day is the sabbath of the Lord thy God: in it thou shalt not do any work, thou, nor thy son, nor thy daughter, thy manservant, nor thy maidservant, nor thy cattle, nor thy stranger that is within thy gates: 11 For in six days the

Lord made heaven and earth, the sea, and all that in them is, and rested the seventh day: wherefore the Lord blessed the sabbath day, and hallowed it. 12 Honour thy father and thy mother: that thy days may be long upon the land which the Lord thy God giveth thee. 13 Thou shalt not kill. 14 Thou shalt not commit adultery. 15 Thou shalt not steal. 16 Thou shalt not bear false witness against thy neighbour. 17 Thou shalt not covet thy neighbour's house, thou shalt not covet thy neighbour's wife, nor his manservant, nor his maidservant, nor his ox, nor his ass, nor any thing that is thy neighbour's.

PSALMS FOR THE SABBATH :

SABBATH : Let us read **Psalms 92** to honor Yah on this day.

Psalms 92, King James Version

<u>1</u> It is a good thing to give thanks unto the Lord, and to sing praises unto thy name, O Most High: <u>2</u> To shew forth thy lovingkindness in the morning, and thy faithfulness every night, <u>3</u> Upon an instrument of ten strings, and upon the psaltery; upon the harp with a solemn sound. <u>4</u> For thou, Lord, hast made me glad through thy work: I will triumph in the works of thy hands. <u>5</u> O Lord, how great are thy works! and thy thoughts are very deep. <u>6</u> A

brutish man knoweth not; neither doth a fool understand this. 7 When the wicked spring as the grass, and when all the workers of iniquity do flourish; it is that they shall be destroyed for ever: 8 But thou, Lord, art most high for evermore. 9 For, lo, thine enemies, O Lord, for, lo, thine enemies shall perish; all the workers of iniquity shall be scattered. 10 But my horn shalt thou exalt like the horn of an unicorn: I shall be anointed with fresh oil. 11 Mine eye also shall see my desire on mine enemies, and mine ears shall hear my desire of the wicked that rise up against me. 12 The righteous shall flourish like the palm tree: he shall grow like a cedar in Lebanon. 13 Those that be planted in the house of the Lord shall flourish in the courts of our God. <u>14</u> They shall still bring forth fruit in old age; they shall be fat and flourishing; <u>15</u> To shew that the Lord is upright: he is my rock, and there is no unrighteousness in him.

OIL MEMORIAL : We must read

the scriptures in Matthew 26:6-13 as a memorial for what this woman has done for Mashiach (Mah-shee-ahk, Messiah/Christ). The scriptures tell us wherever the gospel is preached, we must also tell about the woman anointing **Yahosha`**'s head.

Let us read **Matthew 26:5-13**.

Matthew 26:5-13, King James Version

6 Now when Jesus was in Bethany, in the house of Simon the leper, 7 There came unto him a woman having an alabaster box of very precious ointment, and poured it on his head, as he sat at meat. 8 But when his disciples saw it, they had indignation, saying, To what purpose is this waste? 9 For this ointment might have been sold for much, and given to the poor. 10 When Jesus understood it, he said unto them, Why trouble ye the woman? for she hath wrought a good work upon me. 11 For ye have the poor always with you; but me ye have not always. 12 For in that she hath poured this ointment on my body, she did it for my burial.

13 Verily I say unto you, Wheresoever this gospel shall be preached in the whole world, there shall also this, that this woman hath done, be told for a memorial of her.

THE YAHOAH'S PRAYER :

Reciting the Yahoah's (Lord's) Prayer is a commandment as proven by **Matthew 6:9-13**. Let this be recited by the congregation, led by whoever is leading the prayer.

Matthew 6:9-13, King James Version

9 After this manner therefore pray ye: Our Father which art in heaven, Hallowed be thy name. 10 Thy kingdom come, Thy will be done

in earth, as it is in heaven. <u>11</u> Give us this day

our daily bread. <u>12</u> And forgive us our debts, as

we forgive our debtors. <u>13</u> And lead us not into

temptation, but deliver us from evil: For thine

is the kingdom, and the power, and the glory,

for ever. Amen.

More Hebrew words:

'av (ahv, father)

shem (shame, name)

'ame (ahm, mother)

'Ishshah (eesh-shah, wife)

todah (tow-dah, thanks)

kodesh (koh-desh, holy)

'alleYah (al-aye-Yah, praise God)

alyon (ah-lee-ohn, Most High)

tov (tove, good)

The Holy Bible: King James Version

King James Version (KJV) - Version Information - BibleGateway.com